Original title:
Golden Lights and Christmas Nights

Copyright © 2024 Creative Arts Management OÜ
All rights reserved.

Author: Dean Whitmore
ISBN HARDBACK: 978-9916-94-090-7
ISBN PAPERBACK: 978-9916-94-091-4

Echoes of Laughter Beneath the Boughs

The tree wears a hat, a bit too tight,
Garlands of popcorn, oh what a sight!
Elves juggling gifts with a clumsy cheer,
Santa may slip on that well-placed smear.

Snowflakes twirl in a goofy dance,
Unruly reindeer breaking every chance.
Mugs clink together, laughter on the rise,
Who spilled the cocoa? Oh, what a surprise!

Dappled Dreams of Twilight's Charm

The cat in the tree thinks it's a great game,
Chasing those lights, oh, what a wild fame!
A squirrel steals cookies, then dashes away,
While we sit and chuckle, in a blissful sway.

Frosted windows tell secrets, oh so bright,
As snowmen have snowball fights late at night.
Mittens mismatched, a true fashion faux pas,
But really, who cares under the light's saw?

The Glow of Togetherness

Gathered 'round the fire, tales weave and blend,
Grandpa's old stories, they never quite end.
A dance with the dog results in a fall,
We laugh till we cry, what a joyful brawl!

Ornaments tangled in a hilarious mess,
"Who's responsible?" Just take a wild guess.
Cookies half-eaten, we grin in delight,
As we plan tomorrow's merriment alright!

Frosted Memories and Warmth

A snowball hits Mom, right in the face,
We stumble in laughter, oh, what a chase!
Eggnog spills as we dance to the beat,
The holidays shine with a quirky retreat.

The lights start to blink, like they're on the run,
Singing carols, we all can't be done.
With friends all around, and troubles so few,
We wrap up this night with a fun little "moo."

Soft Glows and Cherished Moments

Frosty toes and mugs of cheer,
As carols clash with friendly jeer.
A cat in tinsel, what a sight,
A dance-off under twinkling light.

Cookies burn, but still they bake,
The house now smells like pure mistake.
Yet laughter rings through every room,
As we embrace the holiday bloom.

The Radiance of Togetherness

Wrapping gifts with tape mistakes,
An ornament that jiggles, shakes.
We aim to hang it on the tree,
But it lands right by Auntie Lee.

Lids off jars of festive treats,
Everyone's sneaking bites, oh what feats!
The dog snags a piece, runs away,
Now he's the star of our holiday play.

Warmth Beneath the Holiday Stars

Chilly nights with laughter bright,
We swap our tales beneath the light.
With marshmallows stuck on our nose,
We sip hot cocoa from mismatched rows.

Fingers stuck to cookie dough,
We bake and spill a little flow.
The mix-up caused by playful hands,
Turning chaos into holiday plans.

Sparkles in the Silent Night

A snowman's got a carrot nose,
Yet somehow, now it wears my clothes!
Chasing snowflakes with delight,
We tumble down, a funny sight.

Under stars that twinkle bright,
We dance and sing in sheer delight.
Every giggle fills the air,
As we weave through winter's flair.

Dreams in the December Air

Snowflakes dance in silly haste,
Sledding down the hill, what a race!
Hot cocoa spills, oh what a sight,
Laughter echoes in the night.

Gingerbread men with arms askew,
Frosting hugs them, what a view!
Trees twinkle like they've lost their mind,
Finding tinsel, oh so hard to find!

Whispers of Yuletide Warmth

A cat in a hat, looking quite sly,
Chasing shadows that sprint and fly.
The fire crackles, it pops and hisses,
While we all dodge the marshmallow kisses!

A snowman grins, carrot nose so bright,
Who knew they'd turn a snowball fight?
Pine needles hug the floor with glee,
It's a slippery dance, just wait and see!

Illuminated Joy

Lights twinkle like a million stars,
Santa's sleigh is parked by cars.
Reindeer giggle, they leap and dash,
While elves tell stories, some end in a crash!

Bells ring out, a jolly sound,
Who's that making the doggy frown?
Christmas sweaters, too loud to wear,
We laugh and tease, it's fun to share!

The Magic of Frost-Kissed Evenings

Frosty windows, art so fine,
Whispering secrets in sparkling twine.
Snow boots squish, leaving silly prints,
Oh, the joy that never hints!

Friends gather round, a quirky bunch,
Table piled high, we all munch.
Baking chaos, flour everywhere,
It's a festive mess, but who would care?

Gleaming Ornaments and Quiet Moments

Ornaments dangling, they swing to and fro,
Caught in a tinsel dance, putting on a show.
An elf on the shelf, playing peek-a-boo,
As cat on the prowl thinks it's chasing the crew.

Cookies all vanished, with crumbs all about,
Santa's sneaky grin makes us question our doubt.
The reindeer are snickering, up on the roof,
They left out the evidence, what's that, a hoof?

Glowing Hearts on Frosted Eve

A tree in the corner, blinking away,
Giggles erupt as the lights start to sway.
Hot cocoa in hand, marshmallows afloat,
A cat dives right in, oh no! There's a goat!

Snowflakes are falling, creating a scene,
While kids have a snowball fight, what do you mean?
The snowman is judging, his face made of carrot,
Wishing he'd gotten a real fashion parrot.

Shimmering Wishes on Silent Ground

Stockings are hung but a dog stole a sock,
And filled it with squeakers, oh what a shock!
Presents are wrapped with ribbons askew,
As I try to untangle this mess with a shoe.

Twinkling and twinkling, the lights start to hum,
My phone's on a charger; oh, what a bumbum!
Tinsel fights battles with the dog and the cat,
While outside the neighbors are singing off pat.

Illuminated Shadows of the Season

Candles all flicker with shadows that move,
As grandma sneezes, oh, that's not the groove!
The fruitcake is wobbly, a sight to behold,
Its texture could rival a hundred-year-old mold.

Sledding down hills, with laughter we bound,
Face-plants in snow make a glorious sound.
With mittens mismatched, we conquer the night,
As elves play their tricks, oh, what a delight!

The Glow of Love Amidst the Snow

As snowflakes tumble, I trip on my shoes,
With laughter echoing, I can't help but snooze.
My hot chocolate spills, oh, what a sight!
But your laugh's a comfort, sparkling and bright.

The carolers sing, but I can't help but hum,
While wearing a hat that looks more like gum.
Mistletoe hanging, I dodge with a grin,
You catch me off guard; let the antics begin!

We chase after snowballs, both aiming so high,
But they hit our neighbors—oh, my, oh my!
In snowman disputes, we bicker and fight,
Yet we end up laughing, all snug for the night.

So here's to blunders and frosty mishaps,
To hilarious tales and silly mishaps.
With you by my side, there's no room for fear,
In this winter wonderland, we spread holiday cheer.

Comforting Light in a Chilly Night

The candles flicker like a dance on the wall,
While we brew up chaos at our Christmas ball.
I tried making cookies, but it's a huge mess,
Flour's my outfit; I must confess!

The tree's half-lit, with ornaments askew,
I swear the cat's plotting to steal all the glue.
There's tinsel in places I dare not reveal,
With laughter and giggles, it's quite the ordeal!

The lights start to twinkle, a sight to behold,
But the neighbor's dog thinks they're toys to be rolled.
He dashes around, it's pure funny charm,
Yet I can't help but worry he'll cause some alarm.

So let's raise a toast to our quirks and our fun,
In this chilly season, we've only begun.
With hugs and mishaps, let our joy take flight,
In these cozy moments, all feels just right.

Illuminated Echoes of the Holidays

Twinkling bulbs on every tree,
They dance and wink just like a bee.
Elves in the corner, sipping hot spice,
Trying to balance, oh, what a nice slice!

Cookies vanish, where did they go?
Rudolph's nose has a festive glow.
The cat is tangled in cranberry strands,
Giggling as he makes his demands!

Sparkling Spirits in the Crisp Air

Snowflakes falling, a slippery mess,
Uncle Joe's jokes? A total excess!
Sledding down hills at reckless speeds,
Finding hot cocoa is all that he needs.

Frosty waves with a snowy grin,
He lost his hat, but hey, let him win!
Singing loudly, off-key but proud,
Christmas cheer in a jolly crowd!

Radiant Hues of a Winter's Tale

Flashing lights and a flaming pie,
Grandma's secret, oh my oh my!
Wreaths that spin and ornaments pop,
Who'll be the first to make the flop?

Gifts all wrapped in clumsy style,
We unwrap them with laughter and a smile.
Tinsel fights with the poor old cat,
Who thinks he's a star in a winter hat!

Celestial Wonders of the Festive Hour

Stars above like glittering nickels,
Mom's got her broom for the holiday sickles.
Snowmen in hats, doing the dance,
Hoping for a playful snowball chance!

Lights that flicker, twirls that shimmer,
A dance-off game that begins to glimmer.
The eggnog spills in a fun, wild swirl,
As laughter and chaos begin to whirl!

Glimmering Nights of Silver and Gold

The stars above are twinkling bright,
While shadows dance in pure delight.
Santa's sleigh is stuck in a tree,
He shouts, 'Get me down, can't you see?'

The snowmen wear a silly grin,
With carrots for noses, and cheeks so thin.
A reindeer slips, and oh what a sight,
As they all tumble in a comical fight.

Hearthside Tales Beneath the Mistletoe

By the fire, we tell tales so grand,
Of elves who tried to cook, but burnt their hand.
The cookies looked great, but took a dive,
When the dog thought they'd come alive!

Grandpa snores, while kids play games,
They dress the cat in silly names.
'Tis the season for laughter and cheer,
Just wait till the cat gives a glare!

Fireside Shadows in Joyful Grins

In the corner, a shadow takes shape,
Is it a ghost, or just an old cape?
With a wink and a nudge, the truth comes forth,
It's Uncle Bob, meant to show his worth!

The stockings hang, all puppies in line,
Each one dreaming of treats so divine.
But one little pup, he jumps up and spins,
While we burst out laughing at the mess he begins.

Celestial Glimmers in Snow

A snowball fight breaks out with glee,
When suddenly someone yells, 'Look at me!'
With a slip and a fall, there goes dear Sue,
Landing headfirst in a fluff of white goo.

The moon above is bright and round,
As carolers sing, then fall to the ground.
In the snow, they laugh, their voices ring,
Celebrating joy in everything!

Dazzling Nights and Frosty Delights

Twinkle lights all around, they dance in the air,
Snowmen wear sunglasses, don't they care?
Hot cocoa spills out, it's a winter-style fight,
With marshmallows flying, oh what a sight!

Elves on the rooftops, secretly peek,
Hiding behind chimneys, they giggle and squeak.
Reindeer are prancing, now that's no surprise,
With candy canes juggling, oh how time flies!

The Warmth Beneath the Snow

Underneath the snow, there's a dance of delight,
Snowflakes join in, laughing, what a sight!
Scarf wrapped around a snowball surprise,
When friendship collides, it's a fluffy demise!

Fireside whispers mix with laughter and cheer,
Stories of snowball fights that bring everyone near.
With gingerbread men missing their buttons and eyes,
In our winter wonderland, what a funny surprise!

Glimmering Paths through Winter Woods

In glittering paths where squirrels do roam,
A deer in a tutu makes woods feel like home.
Frosty the snowman thinks he's a rock star,
While carolers sing off-key, near and far!

Beneath the moonlight, mischief does reign,
Frostbite high-fives every snowball in vain.
Rabbits playing tag, what a wild little crew,
Pine trees are shaking, 'cause they're laughing too!

Enchanted Glow on Starlit Nights

With stars shining bright, and mischief to share,
Reindeer are giggling, floating in the air.
Elves with their hats, all askew and quite funny,
Trying to catch snowflakes, it isn't so sunny!

Whispers of joy fill the chilly night sky,
As snowmen take selfies, oh my, oh my!
Laughter rings out, through frosty-laden branches,
In a world full of magic, who needs second chances?

Whirlwinds of Sparkle and Love

In the attic, presents wobbled,
The cat took a dive, oh what trouble!
Twinkling tinsel danced in air,
As grandma grumbled, 'I need a chair!'

The cookies vanished, nobody's fault,
Santa's on break, let's dance in a vault!
With silly hats and mismatched shoes,
Laughing so hard, we're bound to lose!

Kids in pajamas, socks all askew,
Uncle Joe's jokes—a bit overdue!
We twirled around with holiday cheer,
Spreading our giggles like drinks with no beer!

With sparkling eyes, we'll sing off-key,
A cacophony of joy, oh can't you see?
These whirlwinds of laughter, forever embraced,
In moments like these, our hearts interlaced.

The Ethereal Touch of Holiday Nights

Fairy lights blinked like little stars,
While dancing penguins played on guitars.
The snowflakes laughed as they tumbled down,
Creating chaos, not one frown!

With sweaters too tight and ties like a noose,
Dad trips on the rug, oh what a moose!
Mistletoe awkwardly hangs from the light,
Kissing Aunt Edna? No, not tonight!

The cocoa's too sweet, did someone add spice?
Giggling cousins yelling, 'Oh, isn't it nice?'
Grandpa sings loudly, the dog saves the day,
His rendition of "Rudolph" leads us astray!

Phantom whispers of joy in the air,
As we chase silly dreams, without a care.
We'll cherish these moments, wild and free,
In these holiday nights, just you and me.

Radiance in the Winter Sky

Jingle bells jangled, a cat on the roof,
We watched in suspense, like kids with a proof.
Snowmen with noses made out of twine,
Looked like they're posing for a fun magazine line!

Hot chocolate spills—who made that mess?
Laughter erupts as we play 'Guess!'
Grandma's wig flew off in the blizzard's embrace,
She claims it's a hat now, all the rage in this place!

The sleds go a-flying, oops, there goes Dad,
Right into the hedge, oh isn't that rad?
We hoot and we holler, a festive delight,
In this winter wonderland, everything feels right!

Under the moon, with mischief to share,
We built a snow fort, just hide if you dare!
These moments shimmer, like stars up so high,
In this silly tale of laughter in the sky.

Twinkling Dreams of Yuletide

Our tree's got a lean, it's full of charm,
With ornaments placed just to cause alarm.
Star on the top? It's more of a fumble,
Wobbly branches adding to our jumble.

Ribbons unraveled, where did they go?
A sneaky elf hid them, putting on a show!
Cousins are wrestling in a pile of bows,
Right next to the roast, which Dad never knows!

The carols we belt out, so off-key they ring,
Neighbors are peeking, like it's a thing.
We gather 'round singing, embracing the cheer,
Spreading such joy that the holidays steer!

With twinkling dreams and laughter so bright,
We chase off the chill of a snowy night.
These memories we make will glow years ahead,
In the quirky warmth where our laughter is spread.

Evening's Embrace in Silver Silence

The cat's on the tree, it's all quite absurd,
A squirrel holds a watch, it's really unheard.
Grandma's baking cookies, they fly off the shelf,
And Uncle Joe's telling tales of his elf.

A snowman in shades, he's looking quite cool,
He dances with snowflakes, breaking all rules.
The lights on the house are blinking with glee,
As our dog tries to chase down the wild jubilee.

Noses are red, but laughter is bright,
We twirl in the yard, hearts full of delight.
With snow up our backs, we giggle and shout,
Even the neighbors are joining the clout.

As evening wraps round, in this jolly parade,
We sip hot cocoa, as joy is displayed.
In silly embraces, we're all wrapped so tight,
Under the moon's glow, it's pure, merry night.

Bright Dreams Beneath the Frozen Sky

In the glow of twinkling, the dog's in a hat,
He spins in the snow, we all laugh at that.
The cards that we send are out of their mind,
With the cat wearing mittens, oh what a find!

Frosty on skates, he's flailing around,
As the kids join the dance on the cold, frosty ground.
With laughter and snowballs, the fun can't be beat,
While grandpa just sits, reminiscing his feet.

The chimneys are puffing, like choo-choo trains,
As Auntie's loud singing gives all nervous strains.
"Deck the halls with humor," she sings out of tune,
But we're all in good spirits, like stars, we will bloom.

Under blankets of stars that quietly gleam,
We chuckle and plot for tomorrow's big scheme.
At dawn's early light, who knows what we'll try,
But for now, we just bask in the spark of the sky.

Luminous Echoes of Holiday Joy

The cookies are burning, oh what a smell,
Trying to fix it, we've all gone to hell.
With icing and sprinkles, a glittering mess,
Looks like a raccoon made a big, tasty stress.

The tree's got a lean, it's a haphazard sight,
We laugh conspiratorially, oh what a fright.
Pine needles are rolling like marbles on floor,
And someone just asked if we've shopped for décor.

The kids hold a contest, the best 'ugly' suit,
As laughter erupts in the ring of pursuit.
With lights that keep flashing, we don't mind at all,
Each twinkle is laughter, that beckons our call.

There's magic in mishaps, a joy winging wide,
We twirl in the chaos, with hearts open wide.
With jokes and with jests, as the evening rolls on,
We find in the mayhem, our love's never gone.

Flickering Flames and Starry Nights

As candles are flicking, we start to conspire,
To toast marshmallows, while dodging the fire.
The cat's on the table, swatting the pie,
With cream on his paws, he's the real party guy!

We sing off-key songs, accompanied by cheer,
The neighbors look puzzled, then join in our sphere.
With laughter like snowflakes that dance from the sky,
Our hearts are the warmth as the cold winds pass by.

The lights on the tree start a musical show,
As dad takes a bow, with a grand "Ho, ho, ho!"
With spirits so bright, we're dancing around,
In this wacky winter, true joy can be found.

So sip on that drink with a laugh and a wink,
For under the stars, there's much more than you think.
The night might be chilly, but we're warm and right,
With friends all around, it's a glittering sight.

Lights Among the Evergreens

Twinkling bulbs hang with glee,
Squirrels dance on that big fir tree.
Elves in hats play peek-a-boo,
With snowflakes that stick like glue.

Laughter spills from window frames,
As jolly laughter calls out names.
Even the reindeer join the play,
Wearing scarves, they prance all day.

Frosty pants on a kid who slips,
Using the dog's tail for tips.
Hot cocoa spills, oh what a sight,
But who needs cups when you have delight?

The night is merry, bright, and bold,
With stories of mischief ever told.
As shadows skip dance on snow,
We giggle, chase, and let joy flow.

A Symphony of Flickering Flames

Candles flicker in a row,
As we all stay on our toes.
Someone trips on a festive drum,
And sends the dog into a run.

A cat decides it's time to prance,
Amidst the chaos, it takes a chance.
Laughter erupts, a fiery cheer,
As socks are pulled off, oh dear!

Hotcakes flip; they fly like birds,
While grandpa hears the funniest words.
A marshmallow battle takes the stage,
As we giggle, forgetting our age.

The fireplace crackles, what a show!
As silly stories begin to flow.
With woodsy scents, we share delight,
In laughter's warmth, we spend the night.

Cozy Corners in the Moonlight

Under blankets, we swap our tales,
Of snowy antics and epic fails.
A whoopee cushion squeezed by Bob,
Makes everyone laugh, oh what a job!

Hotdogs toasted on a stick,
Caught a flying marshmallow, what a trick!
Puppies chase shadows, join the fun,
As we light up the cardboard sun.

Outside, the trees wear snowy caps,
Inside, we gather for goofy claps.
Grandma's cookies vanish in haste,
While we all hold our bellies, oh what a taste!

Laughter bounces off the walls,
With echoes of merry calls.
In cozy corners where joy ignites,
We gather 'round, our hearts take flight.

The Radiant Spirit of Giving

Gift-wrapped boxes stacked so high,
With ribbons tied that refuse to fly.
A sticky note says, 'Don't unwrap!'
But who can resist this funny trap?

Friends exchange socks, what a sight,
With patterns that shimmer, are they bright!
A dance-off breaks out near the tree,
As someone trips, oh can't you see?

We trade our sweets, each bite divine,
Until someone sneezes, 'Not that wine!'
With giggles filling the joyous space,
As candy canes fly with perfect grace.

Handmade gifts, from the heart they spring,
Each one wrapped with a joyful zing.
A spirit bright, goofy, and keen,
In laughter's glow, we create our scene.

Twinkling Radiance

In the town square, a cat in a hat,
Dancing and prancing, chasing a rat.
The lights up high flicker like stars,
While Santa is stuck in his reindeer bars.

A snowman's nose is a carrot too long,
His top hat's tipping, he's singing a song.
The kids all giggle, they throw snowballs,
While grandma's still searching for her lost shawl.

The cookies are missing, who took the last bite?
The elf in the corner is blinking so bright.
With icing on faces, they're laughing for sure,
As the dog nearby rolls in gifts by the door.

So gather around for a jolly good cheer,
With hot cocoa spills and good weather, oh dear!
The night is a canvas of silliness wide,
Where giggles and laughter just cannot hide.

Under the Starry Veil

Under the stars, a frog wearing shoes,
Jumps in the puddles, he dances, he snooze.
With each little splash, a cheer fills the air,
While squirrels trade hats, think it's quite rare.

A twinkle of laughter wakes old Mr. Claus,
Who tripped on a present, forgot it was his cause.
With tinsel on noses, the snowflakes all fall,
As the trees start to giggle, they seem quite in thrall.

The reindeer are plotting, they're up to some pranks,
Telling each other how old Bob drank,
A cup full of punch that turned pink from the red,
Now he's spinning wildly, can't feel his own head!

With bubbly balloons and tree bows askew,
They sing all the songs till the morning's anew.
The joy of the night spills out into day,
And frolics of laughter just love to play.

Festive Glow on Frosty Eves

With mittens amassed, and cheeks frozen tight,
The kids skate in circles, what a funny sight!
They slip and they slide, while they're singing a tune,
As a chubby old snowman hums under the moon.

The lights on the houses go blinking and bright,
While grandma's lost socks take their last fight.
The stockings are hanging, all mismatched and wild,
And a cat with a bow thinks she's just a child.

A reindeer is peeking from over the gate,
With a nose like a lamp, it's truly first-rate.
While children all giggle with snow in their hair,
They chuck it around like they just don't care.

So raise up a cheer for the fun and the frost,
For laughter multiplied is never quite lost.
With snowflakes that twirl and a sparkle so bright,
The warmth of it all feels just right tonight!

Lanterns of Winter's Embrace

Down by the river, the ice is a show,
With penguins in tuxedos, waltzing in snow.
They twirl with great flair, quite the elegant sight,
While geese honk in chorus, setting the night.

A couple of bears wear their hats at a tilt,
One's sipping hot cocoa, the other's in guilt.
For the cookies they baked look more like a flop,
But the laughter that follows makes their hearts hop!

As the lanterns all flicker, they cast funny shapes,
With shadows that wiggle like joyful, jolly apes.
The snowflakes above are in quite the parade,
With ice skates on toes, if only they stayed!

So gather your friends for a night full of smiles,
Where giggles and snowflakes go on for miles.
In this whimsical world, every heart finds a space,
To celebrate moments with laughter's warm grace.

A Tapestry of Winter Wonders

The snowflakes fall like clowns, oh dear,
Throwing snowballs and giggles near.
Reindeer prance like they're on parade,
While Santa slips—it's a holiday charade!

Icicles hang like shiny teeth,
Elves are plotting mischief beneath.
The carolers sing off-key, but loud,
While grannies dance, feeling quite proud!

Mittens mismatched, what a sight,
Hot cocoa spills, oh what a fright!
Frosty snickers with a carrot nose,
As everyone slips in their festive clothes.

With laughter bright as a neon sign,
We bounce and skit across the pine.
In this winter wonderland so cheerfully bright,
We share a chuckle till the morning light.

Glowing Hearts and Nippy Nights

Oh, the chill wraps 'round like a silly hug,
And cocoa's warmth makes us all snug.
A snowman whispers jokes, quite bold,
While the dog chases snowflakes, trying to be gold!

Tinsel's all tangled in Grandma's hair,
As the kids scream with delight, "There's magic in the air!"
The stockings hang low, but they're filled with treats,
Candy canes stuck in mischievous beats.

A dance-off breaks out in the living room,
With a twinkle of lights and glittering gloom.
Jingle bells jingle—oops, wrong tune!
But who cares? We'll dance 'neath the whirling moon!

The pie's too hot, bouncing on plates,
As family laughter illustrates fateful dates.
In this cozy chaos, our hearts take flight,
Wishing the joy lasts all through the night.

Enchanted Eves in Shimmering Hues

Snowflakes twirl like ballerinas on stage,
While cats in stockings plot their rampage.
Grandpa's snoring like a festive sack,
While we hide his glasses—there's no turning back!

The lights are strung, not quite aligned,
While sibling teasing is well-defined.
Lights blink like they're having a fit,
And oh look, that reindeer's fallen and split!

Ornaments shimmer, yet one has a flaw,
It's a face that looks like Uncle Joe's jaw!
And Auntie spills punch on her holiday dress,
While we all stare, hoping she won't confess!

Through giggles and grins, the night unfolds,
With stories of warmth and fun retold.
In this bright atmosphere, may we all unite,
In the big, silly love of this jubilant night!

Stars that Dance on Crystalline Streets

The stars wink down like cheeky sprites,
While we slip-slide on frosty bites.
Our breath twirls up in a cloudly twist,
As we giggle at snowmen who strongly resist!

Crisp air carries laughs over every lane,
As penguins waddle in the festive refrain.
With bells a-jingle, we march, oh so bold,
Every tumble shared becomes a comedy gold!

The tree's too tall; it nearly hits the fan,
While squirrel chases down a gingerbread man.
Mismatched socks play peek-a-boo,
Oh ho, what treasures this night brings anew!

Our hearts are tickled as we laugh non-stop,
With milk and cookies stacked to the top.
In this night of jests and sparkling delights,
We'll snicker and giggle until the morn ignites.

Whispers of Light in the Frosted Air

Frosty flakes dance through the night,
Snowmen giggle at the bright lights.
A cat in a hat, oh what a sight,
Chasing shadows with all its might.

Chiming bells from a distant tower,
Filling hearts with festive power.
A squirrel juggling a candy cane,
Who knew winter could bring such gain?

Hot cocoa spills on winter boots,
While elves do their silly hoots.
Reindeer prance in mismatched socks,
Searching for the last candy box.

Laughter echoes in frosty air,
Underneath the sparkling flare.
A dance-off with a snowman crew,
Who can twirl in the cold and woo?

Candlelight Serenades in Wintry Bliss

Candles flicker, shadows play,
Wandering spirits break and sway.
A turkey tangoes in the glow,
While mice host a show down below.

Neighbors peek through frosted panes,
Wishing for ice cream in the rains.
A snowball fight with a twist of fate,
Who knew snow could make you late?

Pine cones tossed like shooting stars,
Sledding down the hills on cars.
Strange fruits hang on every limb,
Carrots sing while reindeer swim.

Frostbitten toes in fuzzy socks,
Toasty treats from creative blocks.
With laughter wrapped in candy canes,
We dance through snow, forgetting pains.

Soft Glows of Yuletide Cheer

Soft glows dance on rooftops high,
While cheeky elves whisper 'Oh my!'
A donut-stealing raccoon named Joe,
Whirls with sprinkles in pure snow.

Fuzzy hats on dogs so bright,
Chasing feathers in the pale moonlight.
A cookie tray gone wild, oh dear!
The munching fills the night with cheer.

Synchronized lights blink in shock,
As squirrels parkour on the block.
Yelling carolers, what a scene,
They mix up tunes, so fresh and keen.

Footprints lead to a snowman tall,
Wearing a scarf, feeling quite small.
With giggles echoing all around,
This festivity is truly profound.

Radiant Nights of Hope and Joy

Radiant nights spark laughter loud,
Silly stories shared in a crowd.
A gingerbread house, wonky and wide,
With frosting secrets tucked inside.

Snowflakes falling in playful cheer,
Snowball dodges bring friends near.
A penguin winks from the icy shore,
Who knew winter was never a bore?

Shining hearts with each shared grin,
Fuzzy gloves on chubby kin.
A snowfall brings a slapstick show,
Along the path of sugar snow.

Footprints lead to mischief's spot,
Belly laughs in every lot.
Together, we'll sing until we drop,
In this season, we just can't stop!

Harmonious Gleam of the Season

Twinkling bulbs dance in delight,
While squirrels plot for a midnight bite.
Snowmen wave with big ol' grins,
Hoping that no one tosses them sins.

Gifts piled high, the cats make a mess,
Tangled in ribbons, oh what a dress!
Uncles snore while aunties bake,
A fruitcake that's tougher than a lake.

Out come the sweaters, itchy and bright,
Parents pretending it's all just right.
A reindeer named Larry, who lost his way,
Ended up at the party, hip-hip-hooray!

Laughter and cheers fill the air,
As cousins declare a challenge unfair.
Who can eat pie without using hands?
The answer is none—dough in all strands!

Radiant Tales Underneath the Stars

Under the glow of the candy cane moon,
Mice wearing scarves break into tune.
The elves are laughing, stuck in their craft,
Turning the cookie dough into a draft!

A snowball fight turns into a brawl,
With slippery slippers that make us all fall.
Grandma's cookies are harder than stone,
But oh, how we treasure that sweet, crunchy bone.

Frosty the snowman's doing the cha-cha,
While Santa gets tangled in threads of panache.
Rudolph's nose is blinking in glee,
As we take selfies for everyone to see!

Under the stars, with each little spark,
The dog starts barking, so we sing in the dark.
Cheers to the season, and lots of delight,
For the merriest moments come in the night!

Flickers of Joy on Frosty Roofs

Icicles sparkle like jewels in the night,
As neighbors compete in the festive light fight.
A reindeer plushie takes to the skies,
While cats on the rooftops plot their prize.

Jingle bells jangle on fuzzy warm hats,
Kids chase down the dogs, turning them to sprats.
Mittens are lost, and noses turn red,
As snowflakes drift down, a soft, white bed.

Hot chocolate spills on the overstuffed couch,
While grandma yells—"Keep quiet, let me grouch!"
The laughter erupts when someone should sing,
Merry notes clash like a half-built swing.

The tree's spinning faster than we can blink,
With ornaments that make us all stop and think.
Who wrapped Aunt Mildred's gift in a shoe?
We bask in the chaos; there's joy for the crew!

Magical Nights Wrapped in Warmth

Fuzzy slippers slide across the floor,
As cocoa spills out, oh what a score!
The stars overhead are wearing a smile,
While mischief abounds for the next little while.

Socks tossed haphazardly into the air,
Footprints of snowflakes everywhere.
Grandpa's snoring competes with the show,
As the cat pushes cookies off with a glow.

Bells are chiming, and kids start to yell,
Pretending they heard, "Hot cider's in hell!"
Sugar plums dance in their head with delight,
As fairy lights twinkle, so merry and bright.

Wrapped in our blankets, we huddle so tight,
Swapping wild stories into the night.
It's the season of laughter, of cheer and of hugs,
With eggnog-fueled antics and warm, jolly bugs!

The Glow of Family Gatherings

With laughter echoing off the walls,
And a cat who's stealing all the rolls,
Uncle Joe's stories never seem to end,
While Aunt Sue's dessert is 'surprise' with no blend.

The tree leans slightly, a sight to see,
As Cousin Tim dances like he's on TV,
The kids are wild, can't sit in their chair,
Spilling hot cocoa everywhere!

Grandma is knitting as fast as she can,
Socks for a grandchild or maybe a fan,
But look at the wrapping; what's inside?
Hope it's not another bright neon slide!

Yet through the chaos and holiday cheer,
It's the silly moments we truly hold dear,
With hugs and with giggles, our hearts feel the light,
In this joyful mayhem, all feels just right.

Candlelit Memories in Winter's Hold

The candles flicker, shadows prance,
Dad trips on toys while trying to dance,
Laughter erupts as he lands with a thud,
Mom's yelling out, 'Watch out for the mud!'

The cookies burnt with a hint of smoke,
Everyone giggles at Aunt Mabel's joke,
She swears that her secret is baking with cheer,
But mostly we know she just forgot the beer!

Lights twinkle bright, oh what a sight,
But the bulbs keep flickering more than a fright,
We blame the dog for munching the wires,
His new nickname? 'Captain Wire-Liar!'

As stories unfold with each silly slip,
We hold those moments, as laughter's the script,
A kinship so warm, despite winter's bitter cold,
Our memories are treasures far richer than gold.

A Tapestry of Light and Love

The popcorn strings hang, slightly askew,
While the dog steals the treats with a light-hearted view,
The kids deck the halls with glitter and zest,
Only half the decorations make it, but they're the best!

Aunt Phyllis arrives with an armful of gifts,
Mysteriously wrapped, she gives us some lifts,
But who knows what's inside those boxes so wide?
Last year was a sweater that she wanted to hide!

With each clinking glass, we cheer and we toast,
To snacks that are burnt and burned eggs we boast,
The pies might collapse, but spirits stay high,
When we make fun of Cousin Bob's pumpkin pie!

These moments of chaos, the jelly and cream,
Make family gatherings a raucous dream,
So we wrap up the night, filled with love and good cheer,
Knowing these memories will last through the year.

Bright Reflections of Festive Spirits

The lights in the yard twinkle and glow,
While Dad's up a ladder yelling, 'Oh no!'
A branch just gave way; now he's hanging by one,
Mom's taking pictures - this is too much fun!

The kids are now yelling; snowballs take flight,
While Grandpa's narrating, it's quite a delight,
He's lost in his tales of how he used to win,
But we just see him chasing the dog with a grin!

Eggnog is flowing, like rivers of cheer,
Yet Aunt Sally's craft has become the town's sneer,
With glitter explosion straight out of a map,
She wears it like a crown, oh, bless her mishap!

Yet through all the misses and festive surprise,
The joy in our hearts is the ultimate prize,
With cheers ringing bright, in these laugh-filled halls,
It's love that shines brightest; it always enthralls.

Crystalline Dreams Beneath the Stars

The snowflakes dance, a funny sight,
They tumble down with pure delight.
A cat in boots starts to prance,
Wishing for snow to enhance his chance.

Beneath the moon, the shadows zoom,
As squirrels plot a gift-filled room.
With tiny hats and wiggly tails,
They giggle and bounce, dodging the gales.

A gingerbread man runs for the hills,
With icing dreams and candy thrills.
But watch out for the sneaky pie,
Who only wants to wave goodbye!

So spread the cheer, let laughter roll,
In childish glee, we play our role.
With silly jokes and chuckles near,
This winter's night brings joy sincere.

Candles Winking in the Chill

The candles wink, their glow so bright,
Whispers of warmth on a chilly night.
A puppy prances, chasing flame,
While flirting with snowflakes, playing a game.

Underneath the twinkling trees,
A mouse in skates spins with ease.
He twirls and falls, but that's okay,
With cheese in hand, he's here to stay.

The stockings hang all full of treats,
While giggling children stash their sweets.
A partridge sings to liven the cheer,
As everyone joins in to lend an ear.

So let us raise a glass of cheer,
To silly moments we hold dear.
This season glimmers, none can deny,
With laughter shared, we all pass by.

A Carousel of Light and Cheer

Round and round, the reindeer fly,
But watch out, they might just try.
To steal your hat, all in fun,
As laughter rings—now, who has won?

A carousel spins, with friends so bright,
Frosty winks under the moonlight.
They all confess, it's quite the thrill,
To twirl through snow, no time to chill.

With each misstep, we laugh and shout,
As penguins slide, it's what it's about.
A snowman craves a dance request,
But flops and fluffs, he's not the best.

So gather 'round, let stories flow,
Of silly pranks, the fun we know.
In winter's arms, we find our way,
With joyful hearts, we laugh and play.

Shadows Played in Winter's Glow

Shadows waltz on the frosty ground,
With silly feet, they twirl around.
A cat in a scarf puts on a show,
While nearby kids squeal as they go.

The light bulbs flicker, shadows clash,
As a snowball fight turns into a splash.
With snowmen toppling, all in a heap,
The laughter bubbles, joyful and deep.

A drumstick rolls, dog takes a leap,
As mischief brews, it's time for a sweep.
With giggles shared, we race and cheer,
Let's fill this night with fun sincere.

So join the fun, don't be shy,
As carols ring, we let them fly.
In laughter's light, we all ignite,
These winter evenings, such pure delight.

Light's Embrace on a Starry Eve

In festive cheer, the snowflakes dance,
The reindeer prance in their silly pants.
Tinsel hangs high, a sight to see,
As Grandma sings, all off-key.

Cookies burnt, but spirits soar,
The cat's on the tree, what a score!
With laughter echoing through the night,
Even the garland giggles in delight.

Jingle bells ring, but who's in charge?
The kids run wild, it's a merry barrage.
Pine needles stick to mismatched socks,
While Uncle Bob tries to fix the locks.

Hot cocoa spills, and laughter roars,
We sing carols, but can't find the scores.
This silly eve, we'll embrace with glee,
As memories wrap 'round like a warm shawl, you see.

The Beacon of Holiday Harmony

A lantern glows, but it's hard to find,
The cat's stolen it, with antics unkind.
Singing off-tune like a duck in a pond,
The neighbors just smile, they've truly conned.

Wreaths on the door, but who let the snow?
Inside we're cozy, but few want to go.
The cookies look funny, but we eat them all,
For every burnt treat is a story, that's our call.

Jingle all day, but the socks don't match,
A backdrop of chaos, an elf with a scratch.
Pudding that's wobbly, like jelly on flight,
We laugh and we cheer on this festive night.

So here's to the fun, and the memories made,
With quirks and giggles, the parade won't fade.
Our hearts may be merry, our joys interlace,
In this wild, jolly space, we've found our place.

Warm Wishes in Shimmering Night

In a blur of lights and tinsel so bright,
We toast to our luck among the delight.
A snowman's hat just fell off his head,
Now he's a marshmallow, sweet and well-fed.

The punch bowl's jiggling, who made that mess?
The dog thinks it's water, what a grand guess!
Santa's got cookies stuck to his sleigh,
As jingles resound in a comical way.

With slippers that squeak and sweaters too tight,
We're all in the zone for this dear silly night.
So come join the laughter and crack up the jokes,
For holiday spirit is stitched in the hoax.

The magic is here, oh what a delight,
As laughter and warmth are our guiding light.
With all of our quirkiness wrapped up so tight,
Let's dance through the evening, till morning is bright.

Stars and Ornaments in Midnight Blue

The stars are giggling in the velvet sky,
With ornaments spinning as squirrels pass by.
Balloons float high, but they're filled with air,
While Grandpa declares, "I could soar, if I dare!"

Tangled in strings, the lights won't obey,
Mom's trying her best, while we just play.
The laughter erupts with every mistake,
As the cat steals a bauble, what a raucous shake!

Our hats are all silly, and tights sometimes slip,
But we round off the evening with cocoa and chips.
Festive hats bob, and our voices unite,
In a chorus of joy that lasts through the night.

So gather around, friends, let's share this cheer,
With our quirky traditions that bring us all near.
With stars high above and love in our heart,
We'll cherish these moments, they're our favorite art.

Winter Nights and Shining Eyes

Amidst the snow, we dance and twirl,
Santa slipped! Oh, what a whirl!
Reindeer giggle, Christmas cheer,
Frosty mugs and holiday beer.

Elves with mischief in their stride,
Wrapped up presents, what a ride!
Socks are hung but with a twist,
One's filled with snacks, did you miss?

Wreaths that wobble on the door,
Cats in boxes, oh what a score!
Chilly nights bring cozy pies,
Stories told with twinkling eyes.

Bundled up, we laugh and play,
Hot cocoa spills, what a display!
Snowball fights and snowman plans,
Winter nights with silly fans.

The Brilliance of Yuletide Glow

Lights that flicker, oh so bright,
Sparklers pop, oh what a sight!
Cats in tinsel, making a mess,
Steps in snow, a wobbly guess.

Fireside tales, we laugh and shout,
Who's that knocking? Is there a route?
Stockings filled with random finds,
Belly laughs and playful binds.

Cookies baked, but burnt on top,
Elves in trouble, will they stop?
Gingerbread houses made with glee,
One just toppled, oh dear me!

Wrapping paper tossed around,
Big dog hiding, oh what a sound!
Laughter echoes through the night,
As we bask in pure delight.

Illuminated Hearts and Frost-covered Dreams

Frosty windows, art displays,
Snowflakes dance in cheeky ways.
Neighbors carol, slightly flat,
Oh dear singers, what's up with that?

Mittens lost but joy remains,
Frosty noses and silly games.
A laugh erupts from jolly folks,
We toast to all the merry jokes.

Eggnog spills on fancy chairs,
Truth or dare brings playful stares.
Mittens puppets, oh what fun,
In this frosty, shining run.

Dreams of sleds and snowy trails,
Cheese platters filled with tasty tales.
Under stars so big and bright,
We giggle through the wintry night.

Gleaming Reflections in the Frost

Windows gleaming, stories spun,
Santa's caught but just for fun!
Snowmen winking, bears on boards,
We race on sleds, just watch our scores.

Carrots missing from the nose,
Hot soup spills, oh how it flows!
Holiday hats, a bit askew,
Laughing heads with cheeks so blue.

Lights all tangled, what a sight,
Who's that shining, oh so bright?
Families gather, jokesters reign,
Frosty laughs with no refrain.

Yummy treats and silly games,
Merry hearts and funny names.
Joy abounds in every glance,
In this night, we twirl and prance.

Colors of Light in December's Grasp

Twinkling bulbs hang high, like stars on a string,
Grandma's sweater glows bright, it's a comical fling!
Elves in their tight suits, trying hard to impress,
They slip on the roof, oh what a merry mess!

Hot cocoa spills over, a festive delight,
Sipping too fast brings a laugh to the night.
A reindeer on skates, oh isn't he bold?
He blunders and tumbles, his story retold!

Snowflakes are drifting, each one a shy sprite,
Kittens chase shadows, a whimsical sight.
A snowman sporting shades, how trendy indeed,
With a carrot for a nose, and he's missing his feed!

Laughter erupts as the carolers croon,
One's off-key like a trumpet with no toon.
But joy fills the air, with each silly tune,
In December's embrace, we find our own boon.

Lively Spirits in the Winter Glow

The festive cheer dances like flames in the night,
Feathered hats wobble, it's quite a sight!
Friends roll in snowballs, aiming for heads,
But dodge at the last, oh, laughter spreads!

Mittens mismatched, a style all their own,
Bouncing around in boots, just like a drone.
Gingerbread men run, with a frosting grin,
But watch where you bite, the house might just spin!

A snowball fight is on, with giggles that clash,
Snowflakes in hair, we all look like trash!
The hot tub is steaming, but wait! What a shock!
The dog jumps right in, wearing mom's fuzzy sock!

As we gather the gifts, with a wink and a nudge,
We slip on the ice, and there's no way to budge!
But through every stumble, we cherish it all,
With lively spirits, we rise every fall.

Timeless Warmth Amidst the Chill

Fireplace is crackling, the marshmallows pop,
Kids trying to roast them, but the batch is a flop!
The cat swipes the treats, a thief in disguise,
While Aunt tries to catch him, with wide, funny eyes!

The carolers sing, well, at least they attempt,
One's off on a tangent, another just exempt.
We share silly jokes, over cookies and pie,
Trying hard not to snort, oh my! Oh my!

Hot cider spills over, in a joyous uproar,
We laugh as we clean up, on the kitchen floor.
The mood is contagious, with laughter set free,
In this warm little bubble, it's just you and me!

Chickens in sweaters, what a curious sight,
Prancing about, in pure festive flight.
With each mischievous giggle, the chill fades away,
And warmth fills our hearts, in a timeless ballet.

The Dance of Light and Shadows

Lights flicker and blink, in a whimsical spree,
The dog's chasing shadows, as happy as can be!
Neighbors hang garlands with flair and with style,
But tangled in ribbons, they sit in a pile!

A snowman named Bob sports a top hat so wide,
He wobbles and leans, with a gingerbread bride.
The carolers whisper, but can't find their tune,
Suddenly sleigh bells ring, and they burst into swoon!

Snowflakes are dancing, caught in the glow,
While kids lose their mittens in the fresh powder snow.
The puppy leaps in, thinking it's all just play,
With a face full of white, he's the star of the day!

We twirl in the lights, as joy fills the air,
With laughter and giggles, who really can care?
In the dance of the evening, with friends by my side,
It's a magical moment, let the fun be our guide!

A Canvas of Light on Frigid Nights

In the chill where snowflakes fall,
The neighbors gather, laughter's call.
With hats so big, and scarves so bright,
They dance around, hearts take flight.

With each twinkle, a playful grin,
They twirl and spin, just like a pin.
A snowman sports a carrot nose,
Who knew frostbite could bring such prose?

Mittens mismatched, boots that squeak,
They stomp through puddles, laughter peaks.
The night is young, and spirits soar,
As snowflakes play, they beg for more.

In this icy realm where giggles reign,
Each warm hug melts away the pain.
A canvas bright, with joy and cheer,
Who knew the cold could bring such beer?

The Joy of Shining Together

A gathering of friends with glee,
They light up faces, can't you see?
With tangled lights, they yell, "Oh dear!"
The cat's a tree, not drinking beer!

Cches stuffed full of cookies divine,
With crumbs like stars, they sip on wine.
A flute or two, they start to croon,
A holiday tune that ends too soon.

Each gift wrapped odd, not quite the same,
With bows askew, it's all a game.
Surprises pop like confetti bright,
As laughter spills through the frosty night.

They chase the dog, who stole the shows,
Through fluffy fluff, a madcap prose.
With hearts aglow, they jump and sing,
The joy of shining in everything!

Echoes of Warmth in the Bitter Cold

When frost creeps up, and leaves a glaze,
Inside we snicker, in cozy ways.
A pot of cocoa, a marshmallow dive,
With friends who cheer, it's bliss alive!

Outside the winds, they whistle tunes,
While snowflakes dance like silly goons.
A rival snowball, a cheeky throw,
Oh dear, that felt a bit too low!

The lights above twinkle with grace,
Each shimmery orb finds its place.
But one light flickers, a bit confused,
It hangs like hope, a bit bemused.

Chasing shadows while sipping tea,
Nothing but fun, it's all carefree.
In bitter air where giggles unfold,
The echoes of warmth make spirits bold!

The Glow of Kindness in the Dark

As night descends with chilly breath,
They gather round, defying death.
With giggles shared and stories spun,
A joke that's told, the best yet won!

With mugs of cheer, they raise a toast,
To those who love, and matter most.
One trips and falls, it's quite the sight,
With snowflakes glistening, all feels right.

A game of charades, with silly moves,
Each bluff and stunt uncovers grooves.
Merriment found in acts so sweet,
As falling snow brings laughter's beat.

The glow extends from hearts so bright,
With kindness wrapped in pure delight.
In the dark where warmth ignites,
They share their joy, oh what a night!

Shining Paths Through Winter's Veil

In the frosty air, we dance with glee,
Snowflakes tickle, oh what a spree!
Santa's sleigh stuck in a tree,
Reindeer giggling, oh who could foresee?

Hot cocoa spills, marshmallows fly,
The cat's in the tree; oh me, oh my!
Snowman with glasses, looking so sly,
We laugh till we ache, time just slips by.

Cookies gone missing, cheeky elves at play,
Sledding and slipping, what a wild day!
With laughter like jingles, we sing and sway,
In our winter wonder, we're lost in the fray.

Winter's magic, oh what a tease,
Falling in snowdrifts with the greatest of ease!
Chasing each other through the frosted trees,
With each goofy moment, our worries just freeze.

Radiant Twinkles of the Heart

Lights in the windows, they're winking at me,
I tripped on the garland, fell right by the tree!
Twinkling laughter, oh such a sight,
Who knew that the cat could fit in so tight?

Baking mishaps, flour on my chin,
Gingerbread houses lean and give in.
Cookies that giggle, oh what a spin,
With every disaster, we bask in the win!

Ornaments bouncing with each little cheer,
Dad's stuck in tinsel, we can hardly steer!
Holiday tunes sung loud and unclear,
The joy of our chaos is what we hold dear.

Chasing the snowflakes that dance in delight,
Slipping and sliding, we howl with pure fright!
Finding the fun in the frosty night,
These radiant memories, oh, what a sight!

Celebration of Lights in Frosty Embrace

Branches aglow with a jolly old grin,
Socks mismatched, where do I begin?
Celebrations booming, oh the mess we're in,
With every twinkle, we laugh and we spin.

The snowman called Bob, he lost his top hat,
The dog made a run, it was quite the spat!
Flying snowballs, oh right out of the bat,
And mom yells "Control it!" but we're where it's at!

Laughter erupts as we slide down the hill,
In our sleds, we shout, "We've got some skill!"
Snowballs and giggles, it's time for the thrill,
This festive delight, oh what a chill!

Gathered together, we toast with hot cheer,
The warmth of our spirits drowns out the cold fear.
With jests and delights, we yell, "Bring it here!"
A merry old season, our hearts filled with cheer.

Embers of Love in the Winter Chill

Snowflakes tumbling like popcorn in flight,
A chair just tipped over, oh what a sight!
Find me a blanket, we'll huddle up tight,
With laughter that melts the heart on this night.

Dinner a frenzy with sprouts on the side,
Uncle Joe's telling tales, a rollercoaster ride!
Grandpa's on the roof, he's taking a glide,
As we share silly secrets, old fears we deride.

Sipping on cider, it's spiced and it's bright,
The lights keep on flickering, oh what a fright!
With friends gathered 'round, everything feels right,
In this winter wonder, love's ember burns bright.

With stories and giggles, we savor the thrill,
Outside it's a blizzard, but inside we'll chill.
The warmth of connection, our hearts to fulfill,
In the chill of the night, we laugh and we will.